Date Due

THEY WON THE WAR

THEY
WON THE WAR

BY

FRANK H. SIMONDS, Litt.D.

Essay Index Reprint Series

 BOOKS FOR LIBRARIES PRESS
FREEPORT, NEW YORK

LIBRARY OF CONGRESS CATALOG CARD NUMBER:
68-58813

TO

ARTHUR S. DRAPER

CONTENTS

★

PREFACE

IT IS almost exactly half a century since General Grant, with Death at his shoulder, sat down to write his Memoirs. Necessarily these two volumes were not a history of the Civil War, for it was not until the close of the campaign of 1863 that Grant became commander-in-chief in the field, and not until May, 1864, that he led the Army of the Potomac across the Rapidan to open the struggle which ended eleven months later at Appomattox.

Nevertheless, the publication of Grant's memoirs did mark a distinct date in Civil War literature. The books published before were manifestly incomplete; those which followed were influenced by his. For Grant was, above all else, the first soldier to see the war whole, to comprehend the relation between all fronts, to coördinate operations about the vast half-circle which extended from Mobile Bay to Petersburg.

After the lapse of fifty years, another American general, who commanded an army larger than Grant's in the greatest war mankind has yet seen, has, in his turn, recorded that conflict as he saw it. Moreover, in one respect Pershing's account is more complete than Grant's, since from the moment the American advance guard landed in France to the firing of the last shot on Armistice Day morning, Pershing was in control: all the great decisions were his, every problem of military policy was solved by him and, consequently, only he knew the whole story.

Almost simultaneously with the publication of the narrative of the commander of the A. E. F., there also appeared the story of the Marshal of Victory. Finally, to the accounts of Pershing and Foch there is shortly to be added that of Joffre, and something of the story of the victor of the Marne has already been foreshadowed. As Petain has written his report of Verdun, and Haig died without leaving any documents behind him, the record is then complete.

Thus, for the first time, it has become possible to discuss the soldiers who won the war in the light of their books, as well as their records. To do this concisely for the reader interested in results but too occupied to examine details, is the purpose of this brief book.

F. H. S.

Blighty, Snowville, N. H.
    June, 1931.

THEY WON THE WAR

CHAPTER I

PERSHING—HE MADE THE A. E. F.

PERSHING not only commanded an army in battle, he also made it. His model is easily discoverable; it was, in fact, the old, familiar West Point foundation with a distinct Philippine Constabulary finish. Indeed, unconsciously, Pershing was his own model. When you stumbled upon a lost American doughboy in a God-forsaken Lorraine hamlet, his bearing, the set of his tunic, his salute, all authentically recalled the general who sat in Chaumont. Frederick the Great's father would have found in this American soldier his ideal of a Prussian drill sergeant. And, in the tradition of the American army, Pershing belongs with "Old Fuss and Feathers" Scott

1

of Mexican War memories. Yet, if he worried about the Sam Browne belt, Pershing was also a fighter, and in the set of his jaw there was a patent warning.

The army he made did not cheer Pershing. For that matter, neither did the Army of the Potomac cheer Grant—or only rarely. Yet, in deference to the soldiers of the Grand Army of the Republic, the politicians twice nominated Grant for President. By contrast, the scouts, Democratic and Republican alike, who sounded out the A. E. F. after the Armistice, came back with the news that for Pershing there was not a vote in victory.

Why? The reason stands out inescapably on every page of his book. He is not a mere martinet. His effort is always to be just, but he is unmistakably hard. Like Joffre, he is also inarticulate, but between Joffre and his *poilus* there was a deep bond of inexpressible understanding to-

2

tally lacking between Pershing and his men. "They do not call him 'Papa' Pershing," Heywood Broun once wrote from France, and the sting of truth is in this comment.

The explanation is even more clearly set forth in Pershing's own narrative in a reference to the First Division. Remember that this was his Old Guard and his Tenth Legion. Part of it had come to France with him, all of it had been trained under his eye. He confesses to a regret that he could not personally lead it into its first battle at Cantigny.

But in the steeple-chase pursuit of the Germans after the final break-through in the Meuse-Argonne, in their eagerness to get up with the fleeing enemy, the First Division troops trespassed upon the area of another unit. In his book Pershing notes this infraction of discipline and remarks that, because of the immediate close of the war, the offense was overlooked. But he must add that, otherwise, some one would have been punished. And this was "his" division.

The secret of the man is in this incident. In dealing with his soldiers, his subordinates, even his closest friends, he was relentless, ruthless; he drove staff, line, and doughboys mercilessly. To fail was unforgivable. Every man had one chance. If he fumbled it, he went back of the line. If he had failed as a general, he might return as a colonel—or a private—that was all.

Yet against this inflexible and inexorable spirit must be set the task Pershing had to perform. German, French, Italian commanders directed armies which had been in the making for decades. Their reserves in officers, staff and line, in noncommissioned officers, which are the backbone of an army, were well-nigh inexhaustible. Even Haig received his armies ready made from Kitchener. By contrast, Pershing inherited nothing, literally nothing. Artillery, ammunition, airplanes, tanks, transport, all were lacking, were lacking to the end. To obtain them he had always to "sponge" upon his allies—the bitter word is his.

Woodrow Wilson and the American Congress had been allowed almost three years to prepare against a war, which was ever rolling nearer. Fearful of inviting a conflict, hopeful of inspiring a world at war by a noble gesture, they had done nothing to prepare for it. Thus, when war at last came to the United States, all was to be done. In a machine age, the army of the greatest industrial country on this planet had to be made by hand. Although war had become the most exact of sciences, the history of the A. E. F. is one long tale of improvisations. These improvisations are all set down in Pershing's book. Since he has no gift of easy prose, no imagination, he has described them doggedly, as he lived them. But the facts are all there for the persevering reader to find and marvel at.

Always, too, the Commander-in-chief of the A. E. F. was engaged upon three fronts simultaneously; with the ally in council, the enemy in battle, and the authorities back home, who could neither appreciate the significance of time nor realize the primary needs of an army in the field. No other commander, allied or enemy, faced quite the same task. Moreover, Pershing did his job.

Unmistakably, also, this American soldier had two of the rare and essential qualities of a great commander. He did not shrink from responsibility and he did not crack under adversity. He discloses the former quality in the single note of conscious self-revelation he permits himself in his own narrative. Describing the emo-

6

tions of the moment when the news of his appointment reached him at his remote Texas post, he writes:

"There never was in my mind, then or at any other time, any doubt of my ability to do the job, provided the government would furnish me with the men, the equipment, and the supplies."

Was this sublime egotism? Not a bit of it. After all, when you have read a soldier's book, you not only know the best of him, but also—alas!—the worst of him as well. No general ever wrote a book more utterly free from personal vanity than John J. Pershing. Nevertheless, the man is in the statement. There is a self-confidence which blinds its possessor to realities and thus leads him straight to disaster. McClellan had it and, although at the outbreak of the Civil War he was beyond question the most accomplished officer in the Northern army, it ruined him. Pope had it, and it took him to Second Manassas. All the German generals had it in the opening campaign of the World War, and the result was the Marne.

But there is another self-confidence, which enables a general to make great decisions, to take huge risks, to believe in himself without thinking of himself. Grant had it when he took his army across the Mississippi below Vicksburg, cutting his communication with Washington before he started. Sherman had it when he set out for the sea. Joffre had it when he accepted battle at the Marne, knowing— and advising his government—that the fate of France depended upon the outcome of the battle he had engaged.

Pershing gave full measure of the same capacity for responsibility in his great controversy with Allied statesmen and generals over the employment of his soldiers. For him, from the moment he reached France to Armistice Day, his duty, his mission, his ambition were all comprehended in the making of an American army which, under its own flag, commanded by its own officers, inspired by a national spirit still untouched by the weariness and defeatism which had already infected all older armies, should in loyal comradeship with its allies bring victory to the common cause.

But in May, 1918, when the Germans were again at Noyon, before Amiens, on the crest of Mont Kemmel; when Haig had told his soldiers they were standing with their backs to the wall and there was no choice but to fight on; when Clemenceau had announced that he would fight before Paris, in Paris, beyond Paris; when the shells of the Big Bertha were falling in the streets of the French capital—the eyes of the whole Allied world turned toward America. Only in that direction did there seem promise of salvation.

At that moment, however, Pershing had in France but two divisions fit for combat and four ready for service in quiet sectors. By contrast, in the camps of the United States were millions of recruits. To organize these millions into divisions, corps, armies, to transport them across the ocean and bring them to the firing line as a coherent national force, seemed impossible within the time it was calculable the victorious and exigent enemy would allow. Was not the single solution to pour these vast American reserves into the depleted but organized French and British armies before other offensives, which were notoriously preparing, should break?

This was the Allied conviction, and Lloyd George, Clemenceau, Orlando, Milner, and Foch confronted Pershing with

10

it át an Allied Council at Abbeville. They did not disguise the issue, they did not mince words. They asked Pershing bluntly: "Are you prepared to assume the responsibility for the result if, because of your refusal to do this, the British army is driven into the sea, the French beyond the Loire?"

For the men who faced Pershing the hour was critical. The fate of France, Italy, the British Empire, the destiny of all they counted civilization, was alike in their collective keeping and in deadly peril. This, too, was the supreme crisis in the life of Pershing. Barely a year before, he had been a relatively undistinguished general officer commanding a handful of regulars on the Mexican border. Even at this moment, he was only the untried general of a still imaginary army.

In this council he was faced by the statesmen and soldier whose fame already

filled the world, whose prestige was unlimited alike in Allied countries and in
America. They already belonged to history; he was still unknown. Moreover,
they were many and he was isolated. His
government was far away. The issue of
the war was at stake. If he stood fast and
disaster followed, that ultimate and all-
inclusive disaster the men before him
feared, the responsibility would be his. He
would be disgraced forever and, what was
far worse, his country would be shamed
in the eyes of the Allied peoples for gen-
erations. History would say that the
cause of justice had been sacrificed to the
obstinacy of a general and the selfishness
of his country.

Surely there never was a higher testing
of will than that to which this son and soldier of the plains was subjected, that day
at Abbeville, while German guns before
Amiens lent emphasis to Allied argu-

ments. But Pershing stood the test. "I have thought this matter over deliberately and I will not be coerced." That was his final word. "It's no use," Milner whispered to Lloyd George behind the door. "You can't budge him an inch." But how can one dramatize the man who, having outfought the Prime Ministers of Britain and France and the *generalissimo* of the Allied armies, that night in his diary notes simply, "Discussion at times very lively"?

In this controversy, which bulks so large in Pershing's mind and book, the American commander was right. He took the incalculable risk and the event justified him. The American Expeditionary Force arrived in time and no service rendered by a million American replacements scattered among three foreign armies could have compared with that of the

13

A. E. F. at St.-Mihiel and in the Meuse-Argonne.

There was for Pershing's decision, however, a far sounder psychological justification than he ever expressed. The French *poilu* was fighting on his own soil. The Germans were at Noyon, before Amiens, about Rheims. In nearby Britain, the British soldier's family was facing slow death from starvation, due to the submarine blockade, and swift extinction in air raids. In Italy, half of Venetia was in Austrian hands. There was no need to explain to the soldiers of these nations their stake in the conflict.

By contrast, the American soldier had come far and cold to a European struggle, the issues in which, so the President of the United States had but recently told him, were without concern for his country. Neither old hate nor present fear shaped his feelings toward the enemy.

14

For him, the German was never authentically a Hun or a Boche.

The American doughboy did not fling himself upon machine-gun nests armed with a bare bayonet, embark in those burning coffins which were his aircraft, grope and grapple in the tangled wildernesses of Belleau Woods and the Meuse-Argonne, to restore the sanctity of treaties or to make the world safe for democracy. Such abstractions are the literary clap-trap of war and every man who has ever shouldered a musket knows it.

But deep in the heart of all these Americans there lingered the memory of the significant sneer which was the response of Europe, enemy and allied alike, to Wilson's "Too proud to fight" speech. Arrived in France, they were instantly made aware of the fact that Europe doubted their courage, the capacity of their commanders, and the resolution of their country. To do an American thing in the face of this foreign challenge—in that resolution was the soul of the A. E. F.

When Pershing saved the American army at Abbeville, when he defended it against so many other similar attacks, he captured a spirit which otherwise would have been dissipated and lost irrevocably. He gave his soldiers their own flag. And for them, isolated in an alien land, assailed by unintelligible tongues, confused by the fog of Old World issues, that was one clear fact, lacking which all would have been an intolerable blankness.

And in the Meuse-Argonne, Pershing revealed the second necessary quality of a great soldier, the will to conquer, "come hell or high water," as the old army phrase has it. There, after a first advance, his offensive was held up as all Allied staffs had forecast. Halfway through the

German defense system, with the Kriemhilde Stellung still ahead of it, the A. E. F. stuck, floundered, came to a dead halt.

Pershing had risked all upon this throw. Again Foch had endeavored to break the A. E. F. into detachments and distribute these among Allied armies. Again Pershing had resisted, and as an alternative undertaken with a half-trained staff to move an army, a green army, of 650,000 men from St.-Mihiel to Verdun and mount a new offensive, all in ten days. Apparently he had lost. Behind his back Clemenceau bombarded Washington for a new general and belabored Foch to bring the discredited commander to heel. Before him was a tangle of forest, marsh, and hill, ten times more formidable than that Wilderness which had all but balked Grant. But in Pershing's spirit echoed the old phrase, "I shall fight it out on this line if it takes all summer."

In his Civil War reminiscences, General James H. Wilson tells how Grant, even his iron will shaken by the carnage and disappointments of the first days of the Wilderness, retired to his tent beside the Lacy House, lay down on his camp cot, momentarily overcome. Outside, his staff waited tensely, knowing well that the supreme crisis, alike in the war and the fortunes of their general, had arrived. But when Grant emerged he was clear-eyed and calm. "It is all right, Wilson," he said. "We shall go forward."

General Allen, in his turn, has reported how, in the dead of night and in the darkest hour of the Meuse-Argonne battle, Pershing, unannounced, burst into his quarters, sat down heavily at a camp table, facing his old army friend, and said: "Things are going badly. We are not getting on as we should. But, by God! Allen, I was never so much in earnest in my life

and we are going to get through." And
they did get through, thirty-seven days in
this other wilderness and a hundred thousand casualties, and then, Sedan, the
Metz-Lille railway, victory! You may not
cheer this man, but you must respect him.

And, in military history it is with Grant
that Pershing must be compared. His
book is far inferior to the Memoirs of the
soldier of the Rebellion. There is nothing
in his military operations to suggest such
flashes of true genius as Grant showed
before Vicksburg and when, after Cold
Harbor, he crossed his army over the
James. He lacks Grant's serenity, that sly
humor which slips out from his page. He
could not have gone to Appomattox Court
House on that greatest of all mornings to
receive Lee's surrender wearing a soldier's blouse and that none too clean.

Nor would Pershing have worried, as
Grant did, lest his beaten foe, who once,

in the old army, had reproved him for slovenliness in dress, should see in his present garb a deliberate affront. Something human was left out of Pershing, and yet, who but Grant, in all the gallery of Northern generals of the Civil War, could have shouldered Pershing's responsibilities and gone forward to success?

To compare Pershing with his peers, the other great generals of the World War, is a difficult task because between American and European military tradition and thought there is an almost unbridgeable gap. The general staffs of France and Germany, before the World War, had literally dissected the campaigns of the past and extracted from them a great body of doctrine and example. Foch, Petain, and many other French commanders were professors of military history before they led armies in the field. For all continental soldiers, war is not an isolated episode, but a science in continuous evolution. The German army in 1914 marched to battle executing the grandiose Schlieffen Plan, which was only the modern version of the tactics of the battle of Cannæ.

Nothing in Pershing's book or record suggests that he ever studied deeply the campaigns of Turenne, Frederick the Great, or Napoleon; his frequent reference to Foch as "a strategist and nothing more" discloses an instinctive suspicion of the "highfalutin" European theories about war. He was not a thinker like Foch in the realm of strategy, or Petain in the field of tactics. By tradition, like all his American comrades, he belonged rather to the ancient and honorable British school of "muddling through" than to the continental, which considered "economy of forces" and other intricate doctrines.

In this respect, Pershing recalls Sheridan. "If it's for larnin' you want him, take Mike, but if it's for fightin', take Philly," the father of the soldier of Cedar Creek had advised a Congressman who offered to appoint a son to West Point. Moreover, in their judgment of European armies and commanders, Sheridan and Pershing were at one. When he had witnessed the decisive battles of the Franco-Prussian War, Sheridan came home and reported that America had nothing to learn from Europe about war.

Pershing was of the same mind. When he, also, came back after another European War, his breast covered with the highest decorations within the gift of sovereigns and states, he issued orders to purge the American military dictionary of such foreign words as "liaison." Under all that dazzling array of medals, the heart of him was still the heart of a "hundred-percenter."

To war, Pershing brought nothing new, and from it he learned little novel. His book and his record are both of the same sort, hard, narrow, dogmatic. He made the A. E. F. and drove it to victory. That is his case, before his fellow-countrymen and before history. But if he was not a great man, there have been few stronger.

CHAPTER II

FOCH, MARSHAL OF VICTORY

IF PERSHING made an army and wrote
a book describing the process, Foch
was the marshal of victory, and his narrative, like that of Grant, is the story of how
a war was won. Moreover, while in the
case of Pershing the book is the man, Foch
is only in part disclosed by his volumes.

In fact, none of the great soldiers of
his time was as generously and variously
endowed as Ferdinand Foch. He had
imagination. Witness the scene in the In-
valides on the hundredth anniversary of
the death of Napoleon. Standing before
the tomb of the great Emperor, the sword
of the supreme soldier of all time in his
hand, Foch suddenly flashed it up to the

24

military salute and in a vibrant voice called out, "Napoleon!" And for a moment the audience—statesmen, diplomats, soldiers—caught by his spell, instinctively leaned forward, peered through the dim blue light half expecting to see the traditional figure of the victor of Marengo, Jena, and Austerlitz appear before their eyes. Always there was a touch of Cyrano in Foch's Cæsar.

In contrast with Joffre, Pershing, or Haig, Foch was articulate. Talking or writing, he had the ability to make great events live. Once, after a formal dinner in Paris, some one asked him the question, "Was Grossetti's division engaged *au fond* in the late afternoon of September 9, 1914?" (the last day of the battle of the Marne). Instantly the Marshal sprang into action. On a sheet of paper he jotted down a map. Here were the marshes of St.-Gond, there the Château of Monde-

25

ment. This was the situation of his army; his right was in ribbons, his center was reeling back in disarray, only his left stood firm. From this left he took Grossetti's division, and moved it behind his whole army, a last desperate gamble to save a lost battle.

As he spoke, you saw the soldiers plodding down the white roads of "Dusty Champagne" under the burning sun. The artillery gallops ahead, unlimbers, blasts the Germans out of Mondement for Humbert. The center is saved, but the left still crumbles. The division should have arrived at four o'clock. Foch snaps out his watch. Half-past four comes, five, and then, at last, Grossetti arrives. Foch addresses the soldiers, the authentic Napoleonic touch. They move out on the national highway which leads to La Fère-Champenoise, disappear in the smoke as the Old Guard vanished along the Brussels road which goes by La Haye-Sainte to Waterloo. Thereafter, only silence and darkness until midnight, and then—Foch's hand swings up and strikes his forehead as if lightning had flashed—a *coup de téléphone*, they are in La Fère-Champenoise, it is victory, the victory of the Marne!

Foch was, too, not only a great commander in battle, but a great student and teacher of war. Years before the World War, his lectures and his conceptions were known, not merely to the French, but to German and British general staffs. He was the first to penetrate the cloak of infallibility which success had cast over the operations of the German armies in the Franco-Prussian War and discover the weak point. Moltke's armies were magnificently organized, but they were not firmly commanded. At Mars-la-Tour, the columns were strung out all the way along the Gorze ravine back to the Moselle, when the advance corps encountered Bazaine's army, not gone as Moltke had calculated, as in fact it should have been, but closely concentrated on the Metz-Verdun highway. Had Bazaine been, not a Heaven-sent genius, but a competent soldier, like Fayolle, like Debeney, like a score of French commanders of the World War, Mars-la-Tour would have been as fatal for the German Empire Bismarck was then planning as it proved for the Third Empire. Half a century later, the same fault would cost another Moltke the Marne and Germany the World War.

On the purely military side, Foch possessed the qualities of Pershing: capacity for responsibility; it blazes forth in his first great achievement as an Allied commander at Ypres and the Yser. He had also the will to endure; he proved that transcendantly in the long and terrible weeks from April to July, 1918. He had one thing more, lacking in Pershing, the Napoleonic vision, the power to see instantly and completely the decisive fact, to answer that question of his, which appears eternally alike in his conversations and his writings, "What is the point?"

At the Marne, he divined by the fury of the German attack on his front, that the original German enveloping movement had failed and Moltke was seeking in the center that success which had escaped him on the flanks. Thus, while his own army was on the verge of annihilation, he hung on and sent to Joffre the immortal message, "My right is routed, my center is broken, my left is firm, situation excellent!"

A few weeks later, in Flanders, whither he was sent by Joffre to coördinate British, Belgian, and French operations, he promptly recognized in the German thrust at Calais the final effort to reverse the decision of the Marne, perceived that to break this attack was to ruin all German calculations on a short war and a swift triumph in the west. Thus, finding the Belgian army almost at the end of its strength and about to quit the Yser, he said to King Albert, "Sire, you have already lost your capital and the greater part of your kingdom; if your army leaves this little strip of Belgian territory remaining, you will also lose your crown." And the Belgian army stood.

A few days later, he learned that Sir John French, his army, (the "old Contemptibles") almost annihilated, had issued orders for the evacuation of Ypres. Hastening to French's headquarters, he appealed to the Field Marshal—he had no authority to order—appealed in the name of the traditional British "bulldog" spirit, persuaded him to revoke the fatal

30

order, to issue, instead, the commands Foch had brought with him. Legend has it that French and Foch, the Irishman and the Gascon, embraced in tears; at the least, it was like both. Thus the victory of the Marne was consolidated at the Yser and about Ypres, and for Germany, as old Admiral von Tirpitz mournfully recorded in his diary, the campaign which was to end in victory in Paris in six weeks, terminated after four months in stalemate in the mud of Flanders.

But it is in the terrible crisis of March, 1918, that Foch's genius was disclosed most completely. While the German masses were pushing onward irresistibly, when the road to Amiens seemed open and the fatal separation of British and French armies inevitable, when the orders of Haig and Petain abolished all hope of maintaining contact, it was Foch who perceived the truth, who at one time meas-

31

ured the extent of the peril and believed in the possibility of averting it. Moreover, so clear was his vision, so irresistible was his passion, that he literally imposed himself upon the statesmen and soldiers assembled at Doullens, seized from infirm hands the fortunes not only of a lost battle, but also of a crumbling cause, and saved the war.

Moreover, inseparable from his confidence as a soldier was Foch's faith as a Christian. In the worst days of the war he would slip away to mass. Clemenceau, arriving in haste one morning, was told that the marshal was at chapel. "Shall we call him?" the anxious staff inquired. "Oh no," responded the old atheist. "Leave him in peace; it seems to do him good."

Characteristic of the two men, also, is the story of their first meeting. Long before the war, Clemenceau, then Prime Minister for the first time, had to name a president of the War College. Foch's name was mentioned to him and he summoned the future marshal. "I must tell you at once," Foch began, snatching the conversation even from the "Tiger," himself, "that my brother is a Jesuit and I am a believer." That was the time when the fight between Church and State was still recent and Clemenceau was the most violent of Anti-Clericals. "I don't give a damn about that," the "Tiger" growled. "It's to teach fighting, not praying, that I want you." And appointed him and remembered him long afterward.

Nevertheless, with all his gifts, Foch had certain limitations. If, beyond question, he is the one soldier of the war who possessed a touch of the Napoleonic genius, who, like the great Corsican, whom he studied tirelessly, could see instantly and intuitively the point to strike, he lacked that other Napoleonic gift, the knowledge

of how, as well as where, to produce the
event of the battle. Tactically he was inferior, not only to Petain, but to many of
his German antagonists, beginning with
Ludendorff.

Thus, with his fellow generals, he went
to the Battle of the Frontiers convinced
of the soundness of the theories Grandmaison had brought to the French general
staff, the conviction that victory could be
won by a brutal, devastating, all-in attack
of huge masses inspired by an immutable
will to conquer. He believed that such an
attack could prevail against heavy artillery, machine-guns, and trenches covered
by barbed wire. That method was the nat-
ural reaction of the French general from
the fatal passivity of the Franco-Prussian War, but it almost lost the World
War in 1914 and did inflict upon the
French army losses from which, as Wins-

ton Churchill justly points out, it never fully recovered.

Two years later, Foch went to the Somme still seeing victory in the limited offensive designed to produce a local break-through. Even in August, 1918, it was Haig who saved him from falling into the old error and letting his battle degenerate into another campaign of attrition on the desert of the Somme battlefield. Not until September, when he launched his final offensive, did he at last grasp the true method, that of simultaneous and synchronized hammering on all the fronts from the Moselle to the sea, which left the enemy no chance to recover his breath or to reinforce threatened areas from quiet sectors. Forty-nine months he spent in learning his trade, and in forty-seven days the Germans surrendered.

Even more striking were Foch's limitations, when he attempted to exchange the rôle of a soldier for that of the statesman. If, in war, he was little less than inspired, in politics he was no more than an obstinate, truculent soldier. Precisely the same qualities which made him great in battle made him impossible in negotiation. After the Armistice, convinced that there was no security for France save in the permanent occupation of the left bank of the Rhine, satisfied that there, in his favorite phrase, was the point, the objective of French statesmanship, he led the fight for this project. The Rhineland, with its millions of Germans, must be separated from the Reich, the "frontiers of civilization" must again be established where Cæsar had fixed them and the French Revolution restored them.

To this end, Foch stormed, expostulated, threatened; denounced all statesmen, beginning with Clemenceau; mobilized the French press, Parliament, even the President of the Republic. All this truculence, all his tirades are faithfully— too faithfully—reported by his Boswell, Raymond Recouly. You see in them the explanation of the friendship of Foch and Sir Henry Wilson. Incessantly, Wilson was pouring forth the same sort of stuff directed against British statesmen, English soldiers, Irish Republicans, until, finally, two of the latter shot him down on his own London doorsteps.

Foch thus raised a tempest behind Clemenceau's back. As for the "Tiger," he had said that there were ten million too many Germans in the world. If he could have abolished them by pressing a button on his desk, as the President of the United States touches off a blast, a thousand miles away, the fiery old Jacobin would not have hesitated. But to annex these millions, to sweep them within French frontiers against their will, that was too much for the man who in his youth had refused to vote for the ratification of the Treaty of Frankfort because it gave Frenchmen to Germany. Moreover, opposed to the project in principle, he was also aware that the opposition of Wilson and Lloyd George made the thing impossible.

In all this controversy, Clemenceau is both the statesman and the friend. On one side he is assailed by his Allied colleagues of the Peace Conference, Wilson, Lloyd George, and Milner, who, angered by Foch's insistence, his truculence, his intrigues, demand that he be dismissed as *generalissimo* of the Allied forces. On the other, Clemenceau is subjected day and night to Foch's interminable barrage. But, although he rejects the marshal's proposals and admonishes him roughly for his insubordination, he saves him, for he cannot bear to see the Marshal of Victory end his career in disgrace.

But Foch is never reconciled, not at the time, when he hangs back until the last moment before going to see the Germans sign the Treaty of Versailles, not afterward, when he narrates the facts to Recouly. Finally, with a total lack of generosity, he commissions Recouly, when he, Foch, is dead, to publish all these strictures, to transmit to posterity the unfair and unfounded charge that Clemenceau, through vanity and obstinacy, had sacrificed the future of France.

Thus resulted that tragic episode. Foch is in his grave, the "Tiger" is visibly dying, the places in history of both, the Marshal of Victory and Father Victory himself, are secure. But, wounded to the heart by this indictment from beyond the tomb, Clemenceau replies in that terrible book, *Grandeur and Misery of Victory.*

In it, he convicts Foch of lack alike of generosity and of gratitude, shows how, after the Chemin des Dames, the battle in which Foch was for the first time in supreme command, when the Germans again broke through to the Marne, he, Clemenceau, covered the defeated soldier before a tumultuous Parliament demanding his head. Standing at the tribune in the Chamber, his clothes still covered with the mud and dust of the trenches from which he had just come, Clemenceau defied the politicians and saved the general.

The blame for this wretched quarrel rests with Foch. Moreover, the details serve to explain something of the bitterness lingering in Pershing's mind when, a dozen years after the event, he sat down to write his reminiscences. It is easy to see how the slow, unimaginative American general would feel when he came to controversy with Foch; what he would think

40

in the face of this Niagara of words, this windmill of gesticulation, backed by a quick, brilliant, domineering mind. Knowing he was right at the time, having been later justified by the result, he would repeat the verdict which the old army passed upon Beauregard. another famous talker also blessed—or cursed—with a brilliant imagination—but a failure. "A strategist, that's about all," so Pershing phrased his final estimate.

Such an estimate, however, falls grotesquely short of the mark. If Foch was not as great a commander-in-chief as Joffre, nor the equal of Petain in the mastery of the tactical details of modern battle, he was, nevertheless, the most brilliant soldier of the century between Waterloo and Armistice of Rethondes.

CHAPTER III

PETAIN, SOLDIER OF VERDUN

No MAN was ever more unevenly treated by fortune than Philippe Henri Petain. A mere colonel, professionally known, but publicly unheard of, he was on the verge of voluntary retirement when the war broke. Division commander at the Marne, his action attracted the observant eye of Joffre. In Artois, the following spring, in the first Allied offensive, his corps got forward farthest at Souchez under Vimy Ridge. In September, he commanded the Fourth French Army in the Champagne offensive, which just missed getting through to Vouziers. Swiftly, thereafter, he mounted to the pinnacle of his career, which was the de-

42

fense of Verdun, first as army commander, and then in charge of a group of
armies.

Then his luck changed. Passed over by
the politicians for reasons chiefly to his
credit, he was condemned to see Nivelle
lead the French army to massacre at the
Aisne, as Burnside under similar condi-
tions had sacrificed the Army of the Potomac at Fredericksburg. Named as successor to Nivelle, after the disaster, he was
condemned to devote months to the reor-
ganization of the French army, shattered,
alike morally and materially, by defeat.

Hardly had Petain completed this task
in brilliant fashion, when the disasters of
March, 1918, brought Foch to supreme
command. Thereafter, like Haig and
Pershing, he was no more than a shining
second. Even when, years later, he was
elected to the French Academy, it was in
succession to Foch, and tradition imposed

43

that his address should be devoted to eulogy of his predecessor.

In spirit and manner, Petain was the antithesis of Foch. Each incarnated the proverbial qualities of his region. Foch was a southerner from the slopes of the Pyrenees, dramatic, voluble, explosive. Petain was not less conspicuously of the north, born on the borders of Flanders, cold, deliberate, not inarticulate, but possessing a fine, mordant, malicious wit, which took toll of all about him, beginning with the politicians, a fact which explains their hostility. To one of these, who inquired complacently what Petain thought of the state of affairs, the general replied: "Not much; today we are neither commanded nor governed."

In all that he said and did, Petain was a "superior" man, and among his equals he never concealed his knowledge of this fact. And yet he knew the French soldiers better than anyone, save perhaps Joffre. He could think of their comfort, their food, their leave trains. Called to restore discipline, after the Aisne, when there was mutiny in the ranks and chaos in the high command, he appeared at the headquarters of eighty divisions in a few weeks.

Moreover, these inspections were no perfunctory affairs. He put not merely generals and colonels, but also non-commissioned officers and *poilus*, on their defense: ordered the private soldiers to send representatives to him; heard them patiently, and restored them to the ranks sometimes literally weeping under the lash of this criticism, but satisfied that the general who was sending private soldiers to the firing-squad for mutiny would spare no malingering general because of his rank.

Petain's army knew that he would never waste a life. His soldiers at Verdun quickly learned that, when he sent them to attack, there would be no uncut wire and their barrage would arrive in time. The infinite care which they discovered in their commander's preparations reconciled them to the incredible sacrifices he demanded of them. Thus, although a quarter of a million fell at his word at Verdun, there were no mutinies as there had been in the French army after the Aisne, and no mutterings as in the British after Paschendaele.

The world had long celebrated the *élan* of the French soldier. The *furia francese* was traditional. But it was Petain who first established the military value of that tenacity which is in the very soul of the French peasant. No other battle in the World War, indeed, in the history of war, was quite like Verdun. And the explanation was equally in the character of the general and the confidence of his soldiers.

"You can rely on us as we rely on you," that was the message which came back from the Lorraine Corps, the "Iron Corps," which Foch had once commanded, when Petain appealed to them to stand and die at the Ravine of Death, while behind them he constructed a line of defense.

If, too, Foch was the supreme strategist of the war, Petain was not less patently the greatest tactician of the Allied armies, in fact, at least the equal of any enemy in this, the chosen field of the German staff. He was master of the new technique, which heavy artillery, machine-guns, all the material of an industrial age, had brought to war. As Foch was the heir of the old Napoleonic tradition, Petain was the pioneer in a new age. In attack or defense, all his preparations were perfect. A limited offensive with a restricted objective, like that at Fort Malmaison, an unlimited defense like Verdun, both disclosed the same foresight.

As a tactician, his greatest achievement was the elaboration of the parade to the German system of attack, that Hutier method which had triumphed at Riga, Caporetto, St.-Quentin, Armentières and finally at the Chemin des Dames. Thanks to this system, the Germans had in swift succession broken through Russian, Italian, French, and British lines and inflicted defeats without precedent in the World War. To the despairing Allied publics it seemed that Ludendorff had at last discovered the formula of victory.

But patiently, systematically, Petain studied the problem, penetrated the secret, constructed the answer. When Ludendorff undertook his final offensive of July, 1918, that Peace Storm, to witness which he summoned the Kaiser, the German shock troops advanced into a desert to meet swift and almost complete annihilation. Thus, on that Champagne battlefield, where he had, himself, just missed a great victory in 1915, Petain three years later finally broke the offensive power of the German army. If Foch later won the war, the foundation of victory was laid by Petain.

Nevertheless, Petain had the defects of his very great virtues. He was essentially cautious, a Thomas, not a Sherman or a Sheridan. Not that, as a subordinate, he ever shrank from any task, however desperate. At Verdun, with Joffre watching from afar, he was beyond praise. But even here, in the terrible days when the Germans took Fleury village and reached the ditch of Fort Souville, he became uneasy. He saw his infantry and artillery adventured dangerously on the far side of an unfordable river, with only a precarious line of retreat, exposed alike to artillery

49

and aërial bombardment. Here was the possibility of another and colossal Sedan.

In this crisis, Petain advised Joffre that the moment had come to prepare for retreat. But Joffre saw the larger aspect. Verdun was already a far-shining Allied victory, a second Marne. For the world, it was destruction of German prestige; for the Germans themselves the denial of hope. To retire at the last was to lose all that had been won at the cost of such unprecedented sacrifice. The struggle was no longer for trenches or territory; the moral value had far exceeded the military.

Accordingly, Joffre sent Petain formal orders to hold on the far bank of the Meuse, whatever the costs or dangers. When a staff officer brought Joffre the order to sign, he called the attention of his chief to the risk that he was running, to the responsibility which would fall to the commander-in-chief, if the disaster which Petain feared should arrive. "Well," replied the soldier of the Marne, "I shall have to shoulder it as I have shouldered so much else," and tranquilly signed the order.

Again, in the greatest crisis of all, in March, 1918, when the Germans were driving hard at Amiens, Petain was satisfied that the attack could not be arrested, that the separation of British and French armies was certain, and issued orders designed to prepare for the inevitable. Haig, seeing the situation more clearly, appealed to London, and the Doullens Conference resulted. In that historic council Foch was named to coördinate Allied operations; the authority of *generalissimo* came only after success, and the Allied cause was saved.

Master of the technical details of modern combat, Petain believed in the supremacy of the machine over the man.

51

Having once restored the French army after a futile butchery, he shrank from seeing it—and France—finally bled white in new offensives. Having at Verdun broken the most terrible of all attacks, he was satisfied of the futility of the tactics of Wagram in the war of position. Moreover, his cool skeptical mind distrusted glowing prospectuses of victory without limit based upon preparations the inadequacy of which he did not mistake.

Pershing, and the American army generally, judged him the greatest of European soldiers, greater even than Foch. The reason is not far to seek. At the moment Foch was endeavoring to coerce Pershing into parting with his soldiers as replacements, he was draining Petain's army of its last reserves. Both resisted the pressure and found a common ground for sympathy in their concomitant controversies with the *generalissimo*. Again, Petain

52

had organized armies and knew the difficulties of Pershing's task. Foch, on the other hand, had merely commanded armies in action and brushed all practical considerations aside with his impetuous phrase, "The battle, the battle, nothing else counts."

Like Pershing and Foch, Petain wrote a book. His narrative is confined to the story of the defense of Verdun and it is, perhaps, the least distinguished thing he ever did. It is a sober, competent, but totally uninspired volume. All the details of the operation are there, but little to suggest the author of the battle-cry of his army, the immortal battle-cry of Verdun, "They shall not pass." Only in chance comments—by a perverse praise of the soldierly view of his antagonist, the German Crown Prince, as disclosed in a book, almost certainly not of the Crown Prince's writing or by a terse comment on inadequate preparation—is the true man revealed.

But perhaps the soldier who defended Verdun justly recognized that no description of his battle was humanly possible. If you stand on the mound of earth which covers Fort Souville and face east, with your back to Verdun, four miles away in the trough of the Meuse Valley, Fort Vaux is at your right hand, Douaumont at your left. They are distant alike from each other and from Souville something between a mile and a half and two miles. And in the triangle between them more than a third of a million soldiers, French and German, died.

The Germans took Douaumont in the last week of February. They reached the ditch of Souville, at your feet, three months later. This was the high-water mark of the battle and from it the assailant was thrown back instantaneously.

Three thousand yards in a hundred days,
a hundred yards in twenty-four hours,
that was the pace of the progress. During
the conflict more than a hundred thousand
shell fell daily within this area.

The attack began in snow and sleet, it
was continued in fog and rain, it culmi-
nated in the burning sun of midsummer.
Within this triangle, first and last, more
than a million and a half of men fought
and the larger part of those who perished
were literally annihilated by high explo-
sives. Forests, villages, even the hills
themselves, were leveled. The countryside
was transformed into that fantastic and
fearful lunar desert of the once familiar
war photographs.

When the French counteroffensive
started in October, the jumping-off place
was a few hundred yards beneath you, on
either side of what was once the village
of Fleury. In a single morning it repassed
55

all the distance which represented three months of German effort. The fact of victory was disclosed to the observers, among others to Henri Bordeaux, who was the historian of Douaumont and Vaux, standing where you are standing, when a French soldier from the superstructure of Douaumont violently waved the battle-flag of his regiment and the sun—not of Austerlitz, but of Verdun—broke through the mists which had hidden the operation and touched with its rays the red of the tricolor.

To the right and left of this front all the way from the Meuse to the Verdun-Metz highway there was hard fighting. There was also prolonged and desperate conflict on the west bank of the Meuse about Dead Man's Hill and Côte 304, from which the American army advanced in the Meuse-Argonne battle, two years later, but the larger part of the action took place in the triangle, Souville—Vaux—Douaumont. Two miles of area, a mile and a half in distance, a hundred days of battle, and more than three hundred thousand killed—that is what "They shall not pass" ultimately meant.

Of Petain it may truthfully be said that he was the one commander, allied or enemy, who made no mistakes. All his undertakings were successful. Even his Champagne offensive of 1915, which failed to achieve a rupture of the German front, inflicted a loss in prisoners and guns hitherto unprecedented on the western front and brought relief to the hard-pressed Russian armies. Moreover, this operation became instantly the model for all later offensives.

On the tactical side and as an organizer, Petain had no rival among Allied generals and in the German camp Ludendorff was his only peer. He was, in fact, the first modern French general—but it is as the soldier of Verdun that he will live in history.

CHAPTER IV

HAIG, "THE PERFECT ALLY"

O F THE group of commanders who con-
stituted the "Big Four" of the Allied armies in the last and decisive campaign of the World War, Sir Douglas
Haig, as the world then knew him, is in
many ways the most difficult to describe
personally and to appraise professionally.
He wrote no book and, dying prematurely,
left behind him no written records of his
military experiences or opinions. Moreover, he exemplified all that the British
army prizes most highly. He shared the
national dislike for dramatic gestures,
eloquent speeches, and, beyond all else, he
shunned publicity.

In the British sense of the word, Haig

had character, but, in that other American phrase, in contrast with Foch, he lacked personality. He was all soldier, in fact, all British soldier. Within that closed and charmed circle, which was the pre-war British army, he was universally and affectionately known, but to the outside world he seemed little more than a shy, diffident figure, magnificent on horseback but less well defined in a council of war.

In the inner circles of his service he had long been recognized as a coming man. He had done well in South Africa and India and even before that in Staff College, his fellow students discovered in him the stuff and stature of a future commander-in-chief. There he belonged to a little group who sat under Henderson, the great historian of Stonewall Jackson. In this group were Robertson, Rawlinson, and Wilson, who were his associates in the World War.

Haig was beyond question a hard and dogged fighter; no commander during the war showed greater skill than he displayed in the great retreat from Mons and again at the Marne. At the Aisne he got his troops across the river and up the slopes to the Chemin des Dames. At Ypres, the resistance of his corps on the Langemarck Road remains a legend in the German army. When Sir John French failed finally and dismally at Loos, Haig was recognized on all sides as the logical successor.

The story of Haig's campaign falls into two distinct periods, the operations before and after the great German offensive of March, 1918. The earlier phase, too, centers on the great battles of the Somme in 1916 and of Paschendaele the following year. And of these conflicts it is hardly possible to speak, even after the lapse of years, without emotion, so great was the horror they inspired.

At the Somme, Haig commanded the volunteer armies of Britain, advancing for the first time to battle. All that was best and bravest, all that was physically and intellectually finest in a generation of British manhood, was gathered under his flag. And on July 1 these thousands were flung against uncut wire, after inadequate artillery preparation, to fall literally like wheat under the reaper in long, even furrows as the German brought his machine-guns up from undisturbed concrete dug-outs and remounted them on undestroyed parapets.

From Serre and Gommecourt to the Ancre Brook, whole battalions disappeared into the blue. Not a few passed the enemy first line, to perish unsupported, when the German barrage held up the reserves. Between the Ancre and the Bapaume Road, the story was the same. Only on a narrow front at Mametz and Fricourt, before Albert, was the outer crust of the German defense system penetrated.

Then began a campaign of attrition, which lasted from July to November. Slowly, doggedly, at incredible cost, the still untrained youth of Britain pushed its way up the slopes, through Devil's Wood and all the once notorious obstacles, to the crest of the famous Ridge. When the autumn rains came, they looked down upon Bapaume and a campaign which, begun disastrously, ended in a blaze of glory in the brilliant taking of Beaumont Hamel.

Ludendorff himself testifies to the strain this operation put upon German resources and the sacrifice of the French at Verdun imposed action upon the British ally. Moreover, the Somme was, perhaps, the necessary school of experience of a people which relies upon the volunteer system for national defense. As such, it is comparable with the Meuse-Argonne, where an even less trained American army made the same blunders and paid the same price. But if, at the Somme, the British soldier of the new armies learned his lesson, the officer of the old army proved less teachable.

The next year, accordingly, the same dreary massacre was repeated at Paschendaele. The German veterans, adopting an elastic defense system, held their front lines lightly and counter-attacked and defeated the young British troops, disorganized by their advance. Paschendaele was like Cold Harbor. But Grant stopped his battle after a few hours, while Haig and Robertson continued theirs for months.

In this battle, Haig broke the heart of his army and lost the confidence of the British Cabinet. The break between the professional soldier on the one hand and the volunteer and the public on the other, so completely reported in Montague's *Disenchantment*, became complete. But to the protests of the government, which knew the secret of the casualty lists, the High Command replied only by the grim assertion that in the strategy of attrition lay the sole prescription of victory.

Lloyd George, not daring to dismiss Haig, withheld from him the necessary reinforcements, fearful of the political consequences of another summer of attrition. The result was the crowning disaster of March, 1918, which cost the British army a hundred thousand prisoners and a thousand guns. The Fifth Army was destroyed and the Germans only missed taking Amiens by a hair.

In this supreme crisis, in the face of a shattering defeat for which he had no direct responsibility, Haig displayed the traditional qualities of his race and service. His appeal to his soldiers "standing with their backs to the wall" touched as deep a chord as Petain's famous words at Verdun. As the old army had stood and died in the last ditch at Ypres in 1914, the new suffered and held in Picardy and Flanders. Haig's troops were "fought to a frazzle," but, reinforced by the French, they kept the Germans out of Amiens and Calais.

When he took the field again, it was a new Haig who appeared. In August he overwhelmed the German armies in Santerre, giving Ludendorff his "black day." He repeated his victory in Artois, a few weeks later. Hurried and harried back to the Hindenburg line, their morale patently breaking, the Germans arrived too shaken to hold this fortress. And, in September, at the moment Pershing was attacking in the Meuse-Argonne, Haig, with two American corps in his assaulting columns, broke through the Hindenburg line at its strongest point, on the St.-Quentin Canal. Thenceforth his advance went forward smoothly and irresistibly until Armistice Day saw the British flag flying in Mons, where the war had begun for its commander-in-chief.

This is Haig's great period and there are those who set down a share of the credit to the arrival at British headquarters of Sir Charles Harrington. In any event, in all the later operations, there was no repetition of the inadequate preparation which explained the massacre before Serre and Gommecourt. But if Haig's success was due in part to a change in staff at least three times in these decisive days, his personal action had enormous consequences.

It was his appeal to London which produced the Doullens conference and his consent to serve under a French general which made possible the naming of Foch. Again, after the victories in Santerre, Foch wanted to press the issue on the field of victory, but Haig persuaded him to strike to the north. Had Foch prevailed, the Germans might have escaped to the Hindenburg line unshaken and the war have been prolonged for another year.

But perhaps the finest page in Haig's military career was his decision, after the August victories, to continue the offensive. Lloyd George, still under the empire of the casualty lists, warned him against all fresh adventures. The British Cabinet told him with all possible emphasis that if he risked new attacks and failed, the responsibility would be his and payment exacted promptly. But Haig took the risk. Believing with Foch that the German armies were crumbling and that the war could be won before winter, he gave his word to the French marshal to attack the Hindenburg line. The result was the final, concentric, combined attack of all of the allied armies, British, French, American, and Belgian, which produced that "knockout" blow for which Lloyd George claimed credit after having almost prevented the delivery.

As far back as 1914, the French had hailed Haig as "the perfect ally." That was in the tragic period when Sir John French was quarreling with Lanrezac, not without reason, but utterly without regard for the Allied fortunes. In that period, when Joffre ordered Lanrezac to attack at Guise to take the pressure off the British, and Haig had agreed to cover Lanrezac's flank with his corps, French ordered him away from the field of battle, very nearly sacrificing the Fifth French Army. A few days later Kitchener and the British Cabinet learned that

Field-Marshal French proposed to take his army out of the line altogether. And that was on the eve of the battle of the Marne! The contrast between British commanders in the first and last campaigns of the war is disclosed in these episodes.

Haig was certainly not a military genius like Foch; moreover, the tactical preparation of his battles was incomparably poorer than that of Petain. By comparison with Pershing, on the other hand, he was a far more experienced soldier, and after four years of trial the British army disclosed in the final campaign an efficiency which could hardly be expected of the A. E. F. in its first great operation.

In British military history Haig will not be ranked with Marlborough or Wellington. His was not an original mind and his method was that of dogged persistence rather than of inspired generalship. Be-

70

yond question, too, he shared the traditional British suspicion of the new and brilliant. Personally he had charm and distinction, but professionally he was at best competent, and at worst, as at Paschendaele, obstinately wrong-headed.

In one respect, however, Haig far surpassed all his great contemporaries, with the single exception of Joffre. Treated abominably by his government, and above all by Lloyd George, forced to accept responsibility for a defeat in the field which was prepared by the politicians at home, refused permission to make the decisive offensive and promptly deprived of the credit for it when it brought victory, he made no public protest.

Even after victory, when popular pressure, rather than official willingness, finally brought him the rewards his services had merited, Haig accepted with every show of gratitude what was offered grudgingly, resolved that no public discussion of the grievances of the general should detract from the grandeur of the achievement of his army. Thus, while history will hardly include Haig in the first rank of the generals of the war, his countrymen will always honor him as a gallant soldier and a great gentleman, and the French people will remember him as "the perfect ally."

CHAPTER V

JOFFRE, THE MIRACLE OF THE MARNE

I F FOCH was unmistakably the supreme
strategist of the war and Petain the
greatest tactician in the Allied armies,
Joffre was not less patently the perfect
embodiment of that thing, unintelligible
to the civilian, incomprehensible to the
politician, which the professional soldier
describes as the general-staff mind.

Inarticulate, devoid of imagination,
without a flash of genius, to the profane
eye, even when he was invested with the
prestige of the *generalissimo*, Joseph
Joffre appeared no more than a dull pon-
derous, unmilitary figure. Thus in the
days of his power he was a legend, and
when he was stripped of command he be-

came, almost overnight, a mere exploded myth.

The public, the press, the politicians, and the war correspondents, all searching for the traits which tradition ascribes to great captains, found themselves completely baffled in the presence of a taciturn, unimpressive general, whose soldiers hailed him not as the "Little Corporal" but as "Papa" Joffre. Once he was gone from the stage, therefore, those who had popularized the legend without themselves believing it, proceeded to destroy it systematically. To Gallieni was ascribed the credit for the Marne, to Foch the responsibility for the Yser, to Petain the glory of Verdun. For the commander-in-chief in all these battles nothing was left but the empty honor of a useless *bâton.*

After the war, summoned before an investigating committee of the French Parliament to explain the opening phase of the war, Joffre completed the ruin of his own reputation. Under the drum-fire of the quick-witted, smooth-tongued Deputies, eager to score off a soldier who in his days of a command had resisted their pressure, he seemed only a confused and empty mind. To the questions of these politicians, trained cross-examiners and famous special pleaders, he could only respond by vague generalization. Thus, he ended by fulfilling Clemenceau's definition of a symbol, "the public man about whom some people still believe what was never true."

So the Joffre myth seemed permanently abolished, like so many other reputations which had lived briefly and died tragically during the war. But then, not suddenly, but slowly, almost imperceptibly, rehabilitation began. It was not due to any action on the part of the old marshal; his silence remained unbroken. It was the soldiers themselves who took up the tale, not merely the generals who had served under him and later become the heroes of victory, but also the German chiefs who had been defeated at the Marne. Kuhl, Kluck, Bülow, and Hausen were far more eloquent witnesses for the defense than Foch, Petain, and Mangin.

Thus, even while he lived in a tranquil retirement broken only by compulsory annual attendance upon the celebration of the victory of the Marne, the glory for which was now denied him, a new Joffre was established in the eyes of contemporary mankind, the Joffre who will unquestionably live in history, for it is the soldier who is disclosed by the records themselves.

Not all these records redounded to the fame of Joffre. On the contrary, it was instantly clear that he had gone to war with totally inadequate strategic conceptions and wholly mistaken tactical ideas. The notorious "Plan XVII" which was the French counterpart of the Schlieffen Plan of the German Great General Staff, was based upon two fundamental miscalculations. It underestimated the numbers Germany could mobilize and thus ignored the possibility of a great concentration west of the Meuse. In the same fashion, it based French battle upon the grotesque theories Grandmaison had formulated, upon the belief that the man thrown against the gun and the intrenchment, unsupported by artillery preparation, could prevail, if only he were schooled in sacrifice and his officers in fortitude.

The consequences of these miscalculations were immediate and catastrophic. On the tactical side, the several French armies were swiftly and completely beaten at Mulhouse, Morhange, Neufchâteau and

Charleroi. Strategically, the French mistake was exposed by the unsuspected arrival west of the Meuse and on the unprotected flank of the Allied armies of the forces of Kluck and Bülow. When the secret of German concentration was finally revealed, the presence of half a million men, the pick of the German army, commanded by the most renowned generals, menacing the British army at Mons and the French at Charleroi, seemed the brief prelude to a new Sedan, destined to destroy the military power of France and the Expeditionary Army of Britain in a few brief days. On August 25, 1914, Allied prospects seemed as desperate as those of France had appeared almost exactly forty-four years earlier.

All who were alive in those tremendous and dramatic days will always remember vividly their emotions, when out of the fog and confusion of the earlier official reports there suddenly emerged the incredible spectacle of vast German armies literally rushing down from Belgium to Paris like some tidal wave following an unreported earthquake. Cambrai, St.-Quentin, Compiegne—all were swiftly submerged. Amiens, Soissons, and Rheims fell without a shot. One day the Germans were still crossing the old battlefield of Waterloo, on the next, so it seemed, they were within sight of the Eiffel Tower.

Then, with equal suddenness, silence fell again. Wireless reports from Berlin and Paris were both wanting. But while the fascinated world was still waiting breathlessly for the arrival of the German troops in Paris, for the promised march past the Kaiser, through the Arc de Triomphe and down the Champs Elysées to the Place de la Concorde, the French communiques, soberly at first, then with an ever-swelling note of exultation, began to record the advance of Allied armies, from the Seine to the Morins, from the Morins to the Marne, and finally from the Marne to the Aisne. Then, at last, the word victory was pronounced authoritatively from Bordeaux, whither the French government had fled. And thereafter the bewildered universe began to discuss the "miracle of the Marne."

But what was the miracle of the Marne? Examined in detail it was no more than the calm, systematic, deliberate reconstitution of French concentration. While French and British armies retired, hard pressed but unbroken, corps were shifted from Lorraine to the Ile de France, from Mulhouse to Paris, divisions were reinforced and reshuffled, the balance of numbers was changed until the German armies, advancing to enfold the Allied forces in their far-flung net, suddenly found themselves inclosed between Ver-

dun and Paris, faced with impending en-
velopment. Having set out to accomplish
a modern Cannæ, a new Sedan of colossal
proportions, they discovered themselves
"out-Schlieffened."

From the immediate danger they escaped. Kluck, with incredible speed and
skill, threw himself upon Manoury: Bülow and Hausen assailed Foch, the German Crown Prince attacked Sarrail. For
four days the issue hung in the balance.
But the German army commanders, lacking in supreme direction, acted without
regard to one another. Thus a gap such
as had opened in the French line at Sala-
manca and the Northern army at Chicka-
mauga, suddenly yawned between Kluck
and Bülow. Into that gap the troops of
Sir John French and Franchet d'Esperey
pushed steadily. Unbeaten in the field,
actually more often successful than otherwise, the German armies were forced to

retire to restore their front. Paris was relieved, France saved.

It is the German testimony concerning this period which actually reëstablishes the reputation of Joffre. What was the lesser Moltke, the German commander-in-chief, doing in all the critical days between September 5 and 9? What, in fact, had he been doing in all the fortnight between Charleroi and the Marne? Between the tremendous tactical triumph in the Battle of the Frontiers and the shattering strategic disaster before the very gates of Paris?

All this time he had been sitting in his headquarters in Luxemburg, a hundred miles and more from the marching flank, issuing futile orders, which arrived too late, were already obsolete when written. Between the armies thus lacking in coördinating control, cohesion was lost, communication impossible. Between army commanders, misunderstandings and open quarrels developed. While Kluck was still acting in the spirit of the Schlieffen Plan, Bülow had scrapped it. When Moltke ordered the impetuous Kluck to cover Paris between the Oise and the Marne, remaining a day's march behind Bülow, he was, in fact, approaching the Seine and a day ahead of Bülow.

In all this time the commander-in-chief and all of his subordinate generals were still under the delusion that the decisive battle of the war had been fought and won, that what remained was only the remorseless pursuit of the defeated foe, a pursuit like that of Napoleon after Jena and Blücher after Waterloo. Acting on the same conviction, Moltke called back army corps to be transported to the Russian front and took them from that flank imperilled by Joffre's counter-concentration. When, at last, the bandage fell from

83

Moltke's eyes, he began a despairing circuit of his retreating armies, disclosing alike to general and soldier the spectacle of a commander-in-chief physically and morally in a state of utter collapse.

Set over against the record of Moltke that of Joffre. His situation on August 25 was far more desperate than that of the German at the moment of the Marne. But the generals who came to his headquarters found him calm, undismayed, his desk cleared, his staff working methodically. Troubled by the situation on their own several fronts, they found in the robust confidence of the *generalissimo*, who necessarily knew all, proof that elsewhere things must be going famously.

Nor was Joffre always at his headquarters. On the contrary, thanks to the diary of a frugal chauffeur who wrote down the place and price of his meals, there was saved for history the record of an incredible Odyssey. He was at Compiegne before the battle of Guise, at Melun before the Marne; he was everywhere along the front where misunderstandings between commanders arose or misconception of orders might produce disaster. Lanrezac and Field-Marshal French quarreled and Joffre removed his oldest army friend. He broke a hundred generals in a week. Did a gap threaten to open between two armies, almost miraculously a division or an army corps would appear marching to close it and arriving in the nick of time. Moreover—and this is the supreme fact— every army commander from the Vosges to Paris was conscious that above him the high command was functioning smoothly, tirelessly, adequately. While the German army commanders improvised operations to supply the lack of central direction, the French carried out the orders which they felt represented their part in the realization of an ordered and coherent plan.

It is the testimony wrung from the defeated Germans which emphasizes this contrast between Moltke and Joffre, the contrast which weighs most heavily upon their minds. For it was at their own game of war that this French general beat them. For half a century the Great General Staff had been constructing a military machine for this campaign. They had evolved a system of war which was to be above the power of genius itself to disturb. They had framed a plan in which, as they rightly calculated, lay the promise of victory without limit. They had marshaled the most formidable army ever seen on this planet, alike in training and in machinery.

At the outset of the campaign, too, they had, according to plan—their favorite phrase—achieved a concentration before battle more successful and more secret than that of Napoleon before Ulm. Thereafter, they had won initial victories so complete as to give them the impression of the decision of the war itself as already achieved. And behold, barely two weeks after this vast host was launched upon its colossal march of victory, it had disintegrated, the pieces had fallen apart, the machine had broken down. The army which was to take Paris was barely holding its own above Soissons. "A high-power locomotive driven by a stage-coach driver," so Foch in his picturesque phrase described the *degringolade*, and German judgment does not differ.

But the world must have its illusion, so the battle of the Marne resolved itself for contemporary mankind into the legend of the taxi-cab rush from Paris to the Ourcq; into the fiction of thousands of the Prussian Guard perishing in the marshes

of St.-Gond, into the Napoleonic manœuvre of Foch, with Grossetti's division at
La Fère-Champenoise. The laurels of the
victor were hastily bestowed upon Gallieni for his vision before the battle, upon
Foch for his conduct during the action,
upon De Castelnau for his defense of the
Grand Couronné, which was the pivot of
the operation. And, last of all, when each
of these explanations proved inexact, the
world accepted the legend of the "miracle
of the Marne."

But there was no miracle at the Marne,
save Joffre. Once, in a moment of irrita-
tion, rare in this tranquil spirit, the old
soldier flung back at his critics, "I do not
know who won the battle of the Marne,
but I do know that if the battle had been
lost, I should have been responsible." And
the truth is all there. It was what Joffre
did between August 25 and September 5
that made it possible for Gallieni, Foch,

De Castelnau, all French generals, to play their respective and glorious rôles in the decisive days.

There was perhaps one other miracle, if one is to accept the post-war dictum of Kluck, who explained the thing in a simple soldierly fashion to a foreign correspondent. Said he:

"We German soldiers knew that troops could charge bravely, fight gallantly, retreat cleverly, but that an army after defeat, after weeks of headlong retreat, could stop, turn about suddenly in its tracks, attack again, that was something we had never calculated upon in all our war games."

So the greatness of Joffre was authenticated at the last. And the victory of the Marne was explained not as the result of a lightning flash of Napoleonic genius, but as the consequence of patient construction, bit by bit, as its architect had built harbor works in Madagascar and railways in West Africa, for Joffre was an engineer. It was the achievement of a man whose nerves were strong enough to enable him to evacuate cities, abandon provinces, even risk his capital, while he was preparing; it was the work of a man who could with equal *sang froid* refuse and accept battle at the gates of Paris from one day to another as he calculated that the balance had shifted and opportunity arrived.

And yet there were other qualities in this general. He picked the men who later won the war. He sent Foch first to the Marne and then to the Yser, even provided him with Weygand, that chief of staff, who was to stay with the Marshal of Victory for nine years and become his *alter ego*, his Berthier. He sent Petain to Verdun. He put Franchet d'Esperey, who was later to conquer in Macedonia, in place of Lanrezac. Moreover, this inarticulate soldier, who was capable of visiting an army headquarters, listening silently to reports and departing without a word, was also possessed of a truly Olympian anger. Those who witnessed his sudden turn upon Lanrezac before Guise have never wearied of telling of the magnificence of the rage of Joffre. In fact, rumor, outrunning fact, promptly reported that he had threatened to send the commander of the largest French army before a firing-squad if he hesitated to obey orders. Yet this was the same Joffre who stumbled and broke down under the questions of a deputy!

The Marne, the Yser, Verdun itself, these were his victories. It was by his order that battle was joined on these fields. His was the decision to accept the challenge. Foch before Ypres, Petain at Verdun, De Castelnau beyond Nancy—all acted under his orders, nor did any one of these great and successful soldiers ever question his authority or deny the fact that they were his subordinates. Moreover, not even Foch himself ever commanded quite the same degree of confidence among his subordinates nor anything like the same utter trust of his soldiers.

Even rehabilitated, Joffre must continue to suffer in history because there is no short and easy way to translate him for a public, which demands that in life its great men shall resemble the statues which inveraciously perpetuate their memory after death. But with Joffre, the ordinary process must be reversed. Knowledge of the man does not explain his victories: the understanding of his victories reveals the general.

He brought to the solution of tremendous problems and to the varied proposals of more gifted minds a good sense beyond exaggeration and, once his decision had been made, he acted upon it with serene confidence and immovable resolution. Thus he was, beyond challenge, not only the greatest commander-in-chief of the World War, but also, as the chief of a general staff, the superior of the elder Moltke himself.

CHAPTER VI

LUDENDORFF—HE ALMOST WON

WHEN one turns from the achievement and books of the great Allied commanders to the record of their German opponents, the contrast is inevitably pronounced. In his portraits of great Confederates, Gamaliel Bradford has memorably set down the inescapable qualities which belong to the narratives of defeated generals. There is so much to explain, so much of blame to escape and to apportion; beyond all else, there is the necessity to explain the impossible, which has happened.

And, in all the history of war, no fall was ever so great or so complete as that of the German High Command. Nourished

94

on the memories of Leipzig and Waterloo,
for half a century after Sadowa and
Sedan, assured of the invincibility of
German generals and the incalculable superiority of the Great General Staff, sus-
tained by the tradition of Frederick the
Great, Gneisenau, and the elder Moltke,
the German soldier not only imposed his
doctrine of the superman upon the world
at large, but believed it himself, unques-
tioningly.

When, too, the history of past triumph
was reinforced by the proofs of contemporary victory, when during the first
weeks of the World War every day
brought the news of a fresh victory, when
Morhange in the west was supplemented
by Tannenberg in the east, when another
German army arrived under the walls of
Paris six weeks after the declaration of
war, even the check of the Marne could
not permanently shake the confidence of

the army in itself or the nation in its generals.

And yet, not only did the German army lose the war, but each of its three commanders was patently, indisputably outclassed. The victories of Joffre at the Marne, of Petain at Verdun, of Foch in the campaign of 1918, which Louis Madelin has named the Battle of France, were due beyond question to the successive failures of Moltke, Falkenhayn, and Ludendorff. And of the three, only the last can fairly claim rank with Joffre, Petain, or Foch.

If Ludendorff was finally defeated, it must be granted to him that he very nearly won. Lee never gave the North a closer run than the Kaiser's Chief Quartermaster-General gave the Allied commanders between March and July, 1918. Moreover the book which the defeated general wrote after the war is not only one of the great and enduring documents of the conflict, but, on the human side, as it discloses the moral as well as the military causes of defeat, constitutes the most valuable of all German war-volumes.

Ludendorff was the incarnation of the German Great General Staff conception of a commander. His was the genius capable of conducting war from a distance, employing armies as if they were chess-pieces, directing campaigns as if they were vast, engineering operations, conforming to blue prints and measurements. In this field, in the days before disaster came, he was the equal of Joffre.

But he was also a battlefield soldier like Foch. In the first days in Belgium, when the German army was held up before Liège by a resistance which had not been expected, when hundreds of thousands of troops were piling up east of the Meuse, awaiting the fall of the fortress to open

the way for the great Schlieffen manœuvre,
Ludendorff showed the stuff that was in
him. A mere staff officer, unattached, he
came upon a brigade which, having lost
its commander, was retiring from Belgian
fire not broken but confused. Instantly
Ludendorff seized the trailing reins, put
himself at the head of the column, led it
through a gap in the Belgian line, took the
citadel of Liège and held it, although at
the moment none of the outer forts had
fallen. For that exploit Napoleon would
have made him a marshal of France.

Thereafter he went east with Hindenburg, began the great series of triumphs
which ended by breaking the military
power of imperial Russia and producing
first revolution and then separate peace.
Russia beaten, he came west with Hindenburg, to discover the German armies
morally and physically exhausted by the
double strain of Verdun and the Somme.

Decisive defeat, loss of the war, seemed possible in the autumn of 1916.

But, in this earlier crisis, Ludendorff's mind was clear and his resolution still unshaken. Without delay he broke off the battle of Verdun, undertook the construction of the Hindenburg Line and drew his armies safely back to this fortress, impregnable then. Thus he repeated on a colossal scale the strategy of Wellington at Torres Vedras and in accepting the responsibility for retreat disclosed the same courage Joffre had displayed before the Marne. Moreover, while the Allied press and public celebrated the retreat as the proof of approaching victory, in reality it wrecked all the grandiose Allied plans of campaign for 1917 and condemned the French to disaster at the Aisne and the British to futile massacre at Paschendaele.

Russia out of the conflict and the German masses in the east released for service in France, Ludendorff in March, 1918, began that series of offensives which brought the Allied armies to the last ditch and the Allied peoples to despair. Three times, on the Somme, at the Lys, and above the Aisne, he broke British and French lines, captured prisoners by tens of thousands and cannon by the hundreds, overran defense systems and reached open country in a fashion unequaled on the western front since the war of position had begun. The troops which he employed were better organized, more meticulously trained, more perfectly equipped, than those any commander, Allied or German, brought to battle during the war.

Nevertheless, final victory escaped Ludendorff. Once more the old weakness of German High Command, the fault Foch had disclosed in his studies of the campaigns of the elder Moltke appeared.

100

Ludendorff could forge a thunderbolt, he could launch it with incredible force, but, once it left his hands, it escaped his control. The system was designed to operate by clockwork, but, sooner or later, the clock ran down. Then came the long delay required to wind it up again, and the enemy, too, had a chance to recover.

Ludendorff believed victory was to be achieved by a single colossal offensive, by the secret concentration of men, machines, and munitions in unimaginable quantities, and thereafter by a surprise attack, striking an unsuspecting enemy with irresistible force. When his first and greatest attack failed before Amiens, he tried again about Ypres. Failing again, he tried at the Chemin des Dames. Each of the three operations was identical, perfectly prepared, irresistible in the opening phase, but beyond the strength of the general to sustain or the soldier to continue to the point of decision. In fact, none of these gigantic offensives was ever precisely checked; in the end, they stopped because of the utter exhaustion of the victorious assailants.

Yet, in June, 1918, after the Chemin des Dames affair, so completely were Allied reserves used up that Buat, chief of the French general staff later reported that, could Ludendorff have mounted another offensive at once, it could have progressed at will. When, however, Ludendorff was ready again, when for the fourth time he employed the now famous Hutier tactic, he met swift, utter, and demoralizing defeat. Petain had found the parade the answer to the German method, and the German masses, advancing as usual, penetrated into an empty desert; their own barrage fell upon a vacant front line, their shock troops were massacred at will by the French artillery. For a second time

German advance to the Marne had proven a mere prelude to defeat, to decisive defeat this time.

Then quickly the disintegration begins, the moral disintegration of Ludendorff, the physical exhaustion of his army. The arrival of American masses has given Foch numerical superiority. At the Soissons Corner, he seizes the initiative, American soldiers fighting brilliantly at the decisive point. Faced with the peril of a Sedan tenfold magnified, Ludendorff escapes skillfully, brings his defeated armies back to the Vesle safely, the retirement, like all German retreats during the war, a model of military mastery.

But the defeat is undeniable, and the Second Marne makes a noise in the world even more disastrous for German hopes than the first. Bulgaria, Turkey, Austria begin to crumble. Meantime Foch rains blows in Santerre, in Artois, in Lorraine.

On all sides Ludendorff encounters evidence that the morale of his troops is breaking down, Allied captures in men, in guns, in territory rival those of the Germans in the spring. Finally, Haig breaks through the Hindenburg line and Pershing reaches for the vital Metz-Lille railway north of Verdun.

Then Ludendorff himself breaks, breaks morally as Moltke broke physically at the Marne. The gambler who has risked everything upon his tremendous attacks is overwhelmed when he realizes that luck has gone against him. He loses confidence in his army, in his country, in himself. Thus he besieges his government to demand an Armistice. His enemy is not yet aware of the extent of the victory. Allied armies, except the American, are as exhausted as the German, and the American army is held up in the wilderness of the Meuse-Argonne. But Ludendorff cannot wait.

The new German Chancellor, Max von Baden, vainly asks for a week, a day, a few hours of postponement. In vain. The first communication to Wilson is launched, and London, Paris, Rome, and Washington know that the war is won, that they can demand unconditional surrender.

But now Ludendorff recovers. While he has been in a state of moral collapse, his army has been retreating, losing thousands of prisoners, hundreds of guns, always going back, divisions melting to regiments and regiments to platoons, but the dreaded rupture of the front has not come. Too late, Ludendorff, encouraged by the devotion of his troops, appalled by the demands of the enemy, calls upon his government to reject the terms requested at his command. Finally he issues an order to his troops, calculated to convince the suspicious Allies, doubtful of the extent of their triumph, of German bad faith.

This is the last military action of Ludendorff. Forthwith the Kaiser dismisses his First Quartermaster-General. Ludendorff describes the scene vividly in his book: William is harsh and his general crushed. They part to meet no more ever. A fortnight later the Kaiser is a fugitive in Holland and Ludendorff an exile in Sweden. Thereafter, Ludendorff sinks rapidly: his voice is raised in shrill denunciation of the "stab in the back" of the civilians which destroyed the soldiers. He appears ingloriously in a Beer-cellar Putsch in Munich, in the Reichstag briefly as the representative of a "splinter-party" whose chief political plank is an indorsement of Jew-baiting. Then he disappears, possibly forever.

Ludendorff's book, like his career, is an irrefutable proof of the moral weakness which underlay the unquestioned intellectual abilities of the most distinguished of the German commanders of the World War. On the technical side, their operations will attract the attention and enlist the enthusiasm of professional soldiers for years to come. They were masters of the details of their trade. They were, indeed, prepared for everything but defeat. When that came, at the Marne, at Verdun, in the battle of France, immeasurable self-confidence gave way to incredible moral disintegration. The tradition of invincibility was so immutably established in their minds that defeat was at the moment unbelievable and, in retrospect, explicable only on grounds unrelated to military circumstance.

After all, the soldier in defeat is the saddest of all human spectacles. There is no defense for him that he can with dignity submit, no matter how gallantly he has fought, how skillfully he has commanded. That is why Lee stands out in history as the most magnificent soldier any lost cause ever had. Returning from the surrender at Appomattox, he said to his soldiers, who crowded about him, their affection and confidence unshaken even by defeat, "Men, I have done the best I could for you." And never thereafter spoke at all. There was so much he could have said. His was a defeat for which the general himself had no responsibility. He could have blamed Longstreet for Gettysburg, Pickett for Five Forks; above all, he could have blamed Jefferson Davis for blunders innumerable. But, instead, he rode silently away on Traveller to immortality.

Ludendorff's moral collapse inevitably obscures his military achievement. Yet only Petain can be compared with him as a technical soldier, and only Joffre as a chief of staff. Strategically, he was inferior to Foch, but tactically his master. If war were simply a matter of machines, Ludendorff would infallibly have won. Perhaps, in *Kriegesspiele,* the practice battles of continental armies, he might have overwhelmed all of his Allied antagonists. But under the strain of actual war and in the moment of supreme crisis the character of the man proved incommensurate with the mind of the soldier.

Thus it was left to Hindenburg, by bringing home a defeated army in orderly retreat, to save the honor of his soldiers and vindicate the tradition of his service.